I STOLE NONNA'S RECIPE BOOK

GERARD HERRERA

LUCIA GABRIELE

*To nonna Elvia ,
without whose collaboration
this work
would not have been possible.*

Contents

Secondi 96

Contorni 122

Dolci 148

Extra content

Preamble

Unable to escape his own animosity, he travels the world in search of some relief. That, he started in Madrid and will end up who knows where...

It doesn't matter too much who, in the end it is one like any of us on the verge of fainting before impetuous routines and goals imposed by who knows who. Moreover, as if that were not enough, he had always fought with what he loved and what he once did sigh of licentious madness : the kitchen.

Between each trip he was noticing that the places, however distant they seemed from each other, ended up being the same, that neither one nor the other land gave him an answer. The trip had become a repeated book and two years of searching had already passed. Almost at the end of day 730, he arrived in Rome and, without his being able to avoid it, a stimulating fever produced by foolishness, the same one that had sent him traveling, the day after his arrival, he was dragged to look for that possible teacher who could teach him the language of Dante.

It was not difficult, he was in the right place : Rome.

He watched his around between pamphlets that lay almost perennial prints on the walls of "Vía del Babuino" street.

"Bingo!" exclaimed the cook.

That little ad, made by hand, delicately written, said without much advertising character :"Learn Italian NOW". Simply perfect, there was the number and the address.

"I found it!", he thought, so without wasting time, he took his oldfashioned papermap and he embarked on the adventure, between alleyways and small squares hidden in the middle of intricate labyrinths formed by that large number of roman roads.

He had lost the notion of time, it had seemed like a couple of seconds to reach the site, but in Rome there is so much to see that couple of seconds was actually an hour.

"Is this the site?" he thought. A house that didn't look right, at least for him, a tiny front door, to enter he even had to slouch a bit. Looking up from him, just after entering, an enormous central courtyard opened up before his eyes, full of lemon trees and a small fountain that harmonized the silence with the sound of flowing water. It was all well decorated, the white amazonite walls, which showed a lifetime among its veins, they ranged from gray to sky blue. Windows with sand-colored shutters and others in darker colors, terracotta, burnt sienna and ochre, all open, so that fresh air could flow into the room. Only one of the windows remained closed.

The cook decides to announce his presence, realizing that no one noticed his arrival : "Hey! Ciao".

To which they reply :"Ciao arrivo subito !!"

"Wow, what a voice!" thought the cook. Without waiting too long, he heard some footsteps coming out, just behind that only closed window, which with certain movements and dexterity, unlocked a lock that divided it in two and thus became a door.

The door opened and the cook, who had so far gorged himself on superfluous experiences that seemed profound, right there he witnessed something that raised the skin behind his heart. He knew that he had not felt this before.

"Ciao sono Lucia", she said.

She was a woman no older than 30, with deep blue eyes, curly brown hair with splendid golden reflections, with a magnificent smell of vanilla and coconut. Her skin matched all the adornments that nature had marvelously provided her.

He said back :"piacere sono Gerard".

From there you can imagine, Lucia and Gerard fell deeply in love. She was supposed to be his Italian teacher, but ended up being his girlfriend.

After a couple of months, Lucia proposes to Gerard to go visit her family.

This guy, who up to now was known to us as "the cook", we discovered his name is Gerard.

He was thus summoned to a meeting with the "Famiglia".

Lucia's family lives in a town near Rome called Arpino. That's where everything happens, there, right there, is where Gerard meets that woman who becomes the protagonist of this story.

Because Lucia and Gerard are just part of the cast, so without any more preambles, the history!

Nonna's recipe book

Arriving , I found a place covered with green mountains, with streams that cross the streets, with natural stone walls.

Houses that match their surroundings, flowers that climb up the walls of the buildings and intertwine in the windows to adorn those beautiful mansions.

Right there, almost without warning, was Nonna's house.

It was not necessary to knock on the door, she had already noticed our arrival from the upper floor.

In a very cordial way she opened the door with a big smile, a hug followed by two kisses.

They start with the left cheek to the right one, which confused me so much, because it is done in the opposite way in Spain, there are two kisses and they start with the right cheek to the left one.

La Nonna : calm, patient and with a pure look. A simple woman, petite but strong, all her hair the color of pearl and a huge and immaculate smile. She thus invited us to come in and sit at a small table that is right inside the kitchen, where everything happens, baptisms and weddings, celebrations or the simplicity of family daily life.

While la Nonna and Lucia talked about a little bit of everything, la Nonna took advantage of pauses in the conversation to give me scrutinizing glances. Other times, she simply touched like anyone who touches her most beloved pet, a striking little book, she always had it within reach of her hand. Only then did I notice the existence of that filigree notebook.

"Is it a recipe book?" I asked.

While I tried to get it closer to me, she grabbed it tightly with one hand and with the other she pulled me away severely.

I thought : "Wow, my first meeting was not what I expected!".

Nonna looked at me with such annoyance, immediately disapproving of my inappropriate way of approaching her; without any words, it was only that look that spoke. I felt absurdly moved, as if something terribly had happened, so at least it seemed, Lucia tried to lighten the atmosphere, asking her a couple of questions about another argument.

However something much deeper had made presence in me, the emotions had diminished, so the clarity made me notice that powerful curiosity. How much I would like to know what is behind that little book, but it was not possible for me to find out what was contained in that beautiful notebook with fine details, gold and silver threads that decorated its cover.

I could only see what I could discover at least 5 meters away, it has a drawing in the main part, like a sort of ancient Chinese porcelain itself, with flowers and aged colors. A design almost made to be perfected over the years, cracks that split the paint and the gold threads, in thousands of works of art, which at the same time final is only one, one that contains something of greater value than what its own cover shows.

I knew that as soon as I tried to approach that folder again, her owner would hastily hide it in the pockets of her dress, as she had done before, or even in more remote places, of course thus making it inaccessible to me.

La Nonna seemed to have installed in her primary sensors a kind of alarm that warned her of my presence, every day when it was time for our usual visit.

As a routine, Lucía and I decided to go to Nonna's house between 5 and 7 in the afternoon. She, the Nonna, found her protocol activated, even when I approached from the most absolute silence to the table where the beautiful golden book rested, she, with a supernatural power, perceived my energy, even my intentions and with only one look at me glared.

The more she protected it, the greater was my curiosity to find out what that recipe book contained.

Tempting mystery! What was in that bundle of pages? Spell recipes? Magical affairs? Essences or healing potions? If it contained any of these supernatural things? Is that why the concealment came? Was it perhaps covering up some family secret, was it a diary perhaps? The formula of eternal life?

Impossible! Such things are either taken much closer, or guarded much further away: either they lie in the heart or they are filed away in a well-closed, secure file.

It will be then that it was the remains of loving stories from her youth that calmed down in those hundred pages, full of pages yellowed by the passing of decades, those that rust the days.

Now I give you the ability to judge me, because you already have it and it's yours, so those incapable of following the true value of curiosity, criticize my conduct as you like. Call me crazy, capricious, indiscreet, and, for the sake of it, meddlesome and impertinent snooper .

The truth is that this recipe book made me reckless, and without the legitimate means, I put into play the transgressive, and heroic ones.

Look at me as a madman! When I was close to that recipe book my skin became a radio antenna, almost seeking to tune in to the frequency of everything that was contained in those pages.

How much the idea of knowing that secret inflamed me, when only I was pursuing the satisfaction of curiosity.

And luck, what would deny me victory? If victory really mattered to me, I'd grant it to myself... and by granting it, I felt remorse.

After the seventh week of that compulsive obsession, I returned with a glimpse of sanity, with a bitter taste in all my senses, I had returned from a night of 24 and a half hours, those of tormenting dreams.

I felt the repugnance and behavior of a jerk himself, that unusual little book, made me fight with myself like a man with two heads, and also, already exalted in my own esteem (for lack of another sweeter and deeper exaltation), I understood my guilt and wallowed even deeper in it. So I asked for a loan from the affection and only the affection of the beautiful key named Lucia, throughout this story, la Nonna, without any fear of the jealousy of her other grandchildren, showed her preference for Lucia, my girlfriend, it was obvious.

So for this, I insisted, I surpassed myself, I deployed all the resources, and like the artist who cultivates inspiration through discipline, I reached such a degree of mastery in manipulation, so I used love as an excuse to that Lucia for love insisted on Nonna for love and I would be profited by such an act of impugnable greed. So, my persuasion would make possible my encounter with the content contained in that notebook, that secret that had already possessed me.

If you are reading this book that is now in your hands, you will know if my master plan worked or not...

Neither Nonna was forced, nor was she sentenced to the simple curiosity of a stunned Chef. No, neither Lucia was manipulated nor I, this writer, took advantage of nothing, corrupted someone or filled his hidden desires with needs.

Nonna, with her unconditional love for cooking, taught us all these recipes that I offer you in the next pages, of a historical nature in her life. In the life of that 90-year-old Lady, and, in the life of those who inhabit for this pristine italian region, called Lazio, full of seasonal products, between mountains that cover and fill the widest wild vegetation that becomes food that amazes our senses.

Each season offers us the available recipe book, a natural recipe book, because yes, it is nature, the pantry and the supermarket in this region.
It is a cuisine considered poor, but only from a superfluous comparison or perhaps by those who profess it with great humility, so they do not load it with expectations or competitiveness, its true and purest essence, that is Ciociara cuisine...

CIOCIARIA

Ciociaria is a historic region in the heart of Lazio, located halfway between Rome (north) and Naples (south).

The name of this land is closely linked to the Lazio footwear called "ciocie". Traditional footwear used by shepherds, it was perhaps the first product of the Ciociaria handicraft. Made with bovine and sheep skins, they were robust and suitable for walking on tilled fields and on steep paths. Arpino is the town that still produces them by hand today.

The traditional Ciociara cuisine is linked to the activity that its inhabitants have always carried out: sheep farming and agriculture. Despite the transformations due to modern life, the Ciociaria retains vivid memories of that simple and authentic peasant life, of that hard work and of the life that its inhabitants lived with stubbornness, enthusiasm, creativity and hospitality.

The strong point of the Ciociara cuisine is the essentiality and genuineness of its products, given by the excellent agricultural resources of the area: cereals, vegetables, vineyards, olive trees and sheep-farming products.

ANTIPASTI

CALASCIONI

Calascioni are a kind of very tasty empanadas typical of the Lazio region, in particular of the Ciociaria area. Traditionally they are prepared around Easter time, but they are excellent at any time of year!

INGREDIENTS

Serving size for 10 - 12 calascioni

For the dough :

200 g of 00 flour (7oz)

2 eggs (room temperature)

1 tablespoon of extra virgin olive oil

1 pinch of fine salt

For the filling :

175 g of grated pecorino romano (6oz)

150 g of dry pork sausage (5oz)

2 eggs (room temperature)

1 egg yolk (to brush the surface)

DIRECTION

Pour the flour into a bowl, add the two eggs, a pinch of salt and a spoonful of extra virgin olive oil. Start mixing with your hand, mixing all the ingredients well until compact.

Turn the compound obtained onto the work surface and knead it for about 10 minutes, until you obtain a soft and elastic ball - or loaf - then wrap it in transparent film and let it rest for at least 20 minutes. In the meantime, take care of the filling: break the two eggs in a bowl and beat them lightly, then add the pecorino romano. Season with salt and pepper and mix, obtaining a creamy and fairly dry (but not dry) mixture. Peel and slice the dried sausage, then cut it into small cubes which you will add to the mixture, mixing everything together. Take the dough ball, unwrap it and roll it out on a lightly floured table. The thickness should be around 4-5 millimeters (half a centimeter, no more). With a pastry cutter of ten centimeters in diameter, make many discs, re-knead the leftover dough, roll it out again and make other discs.

Important: while rolling out the dough, never add flour and I recommend not putting too much stuffing inside, because the egg will swell as it cooks and could leak.

Take a mound of dough and place it in the center of the disc, brush the edges and close in a half-moon shape, pressing very well along the edges so as to prevent them from opening during cooking. Once sealed, you can also go through them again with the fork prongs.

Continue like this until you have completed all the calascioni, which you will have gradually placed in a baking tray lined with parchment paper.

Lightly beat an egg yolk and brush the surface of all the calascioni.

Heat the oven to 180°C (356 °F).

As soon as the oven reaches the temperature, put the calascioni in the oven and cook for about 20 minutes at 180°C (356 °F). The cooking time can vary depending on your oven, from a minimum of 15 minutes to a maximum of 20-25, so always check your calascioni while they are cooking: they must be well browned and puffy.

Take the Calascioni Ciociari out of the oven, let them cool down and enjoy them right away!

RUSTIC PIZZA

FILLED WITH TURNIP TOPS

INGREDIENTS

Serving size for 10 people

FOR THE DOUGH :

550 g of flour (1lb 4oz)
1 glass of white wine
1 glass of extra virgin olive oil
1 pinch of salt

FOR THE FILLING :

350 g (cooked) of chicory or turnip tops (12 oz)
10 black olives
200 g of dry sausage (7 oz)

DIRECTION

Work the dough very well until you get a homogeneous dough, let it rest for an hour in the refrigerator. Then divide the dough into two parts. Roll out one of these parts very thin and cover a buttered pan with it. In a pan put extra virgin olive oil with garlic and fry the vegetables. Add the black olives cut into small pieces and the sausage into small pieces. Pour the filling into the pan over the first layer of dough and roll it out. Take the second loaf of dough, roll it out very thin and place it on the vegetable filling, closing well by folding the edges of the dough. Pierce the top layer of the cake with a fork. Brush the surface with an egg yolk. Set the static oven at 180° (356 °F), if ventilated at 170° (338 °F) for 50 minutes.

BRUSCHETTE CIOCIARE

WITH PEPPERS

To share

INGREDIENTS:

8 slices of bread
1 large pepper
1 large clove of garlic
a handful of desalted capers
basil, salt and oil to taste

DIRECTION

Roast the peppers on the grill. Once ready, place them in a plastic bag for food for a few minutes: this will facilitate the peeling phase. Once cooled, remove them from the bag, peel them and cut them into strips.

Separately, cut the garlic into slices and mince it, rinse the capers, mince the basil, add them to the peppers with oil and salt and mix to flavor.

Cut the stale bread into slices that are not too thick and toast them on the grill or in the oven, until golden brown. As soon as the bread is toasted, arrange the slices in a serving dish and season them with the peppers.

You can enrich the bruschetta with peppers with black olives, tomatoes and onion or with the addition of anchovies. You can also make the condiment more aromatic by adding balsamic vinegar.

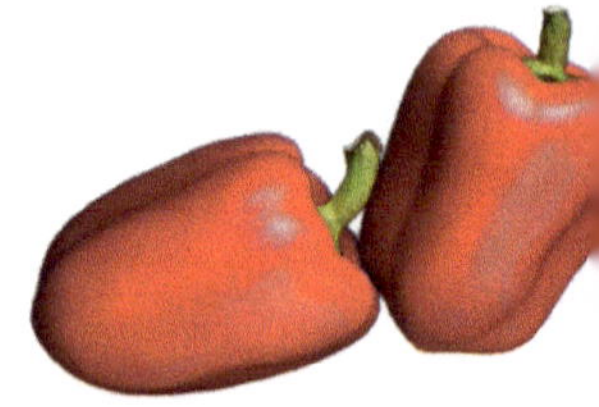

WITH CERRY TOMATOES AND BASIL

To share

INGREDIENTS

8 slices of bread
10 to 15 cherry tomatoes
7 large leaves of basil
1 clove of garlic
a tablespoon of oil
oregano, salt and pepper to taste

DIRECTION

Wash and dry the cherry tomatoes , cut them into chunks and put them in a bowl with the chopped basil leaves, oregano, salt and pepper.

Dress with a spoonful of extra virgin olive oil. Let it infuse for 20 minutes.

Brush the side of the bruschetta to be filled with oil and then toast the bread on both sides. You can use the oven or the non-stick pan.

Rub the peeled garlic clove on each bruschetta and distribute the seasoned tomato on the still warm bruschetta.

Leave to rest for a minute and serve while still hot.

WITH GRILLED EGGPLANTS

To share

INGREDIENTS

8 slices of bread
2 medium eggplants
2 tablespoon of oil
3 cloves of garlic
a handful of parsley
a pinch of salt

DIRECTION

Wash the eggplants, remove the stem and peel. Cut them into slices and grill them. Prepare a mixture with oil, parsley and garlic.

Pour it over the eggplants, add a little salt and let it infuse. Cut the slices of bread to a thickness of about half a centimeter.

Toast them over the coals or in the oven, then take them out of the oven and spread the eggplants on the bruschetta.

WITH PORCINI MUSHROOMS

To share

INGREDIENTS

8 slices of bread
11 oz of porcini mushrooms
1 small clove of garlic
1 tablespoon of oil
a small handful of parsley
salt and pepper to taste

DIRECTION

First, clean the porcini mushrooms well with a damp kitchen cloth in order to eliminate the earth residues. Once cleaned, cut them into small pieces.

In a pan put the oil and the sliced clove of garlic, whoever prefers can crush it. Once the garlic is golden, add the mushrooms and brown them over medium heat. Then add the chopped parsley, salt and pepper. Cook for about ten minutes, stirring frequently to prevent them from sticking to the pan.

Cut the bread into slices, put them on a dripping pan with a drizzle of oil and toast in the oven at medium temperature for 10 minutes, or until golden brown, turning the slices halfway through cooking.

As soon as the bread is ready, dress it immediately with the porcini mushrooms and serve, perhaps adding another sprinkling of parsley.

FRIED CIOCIARI APPETIZERS

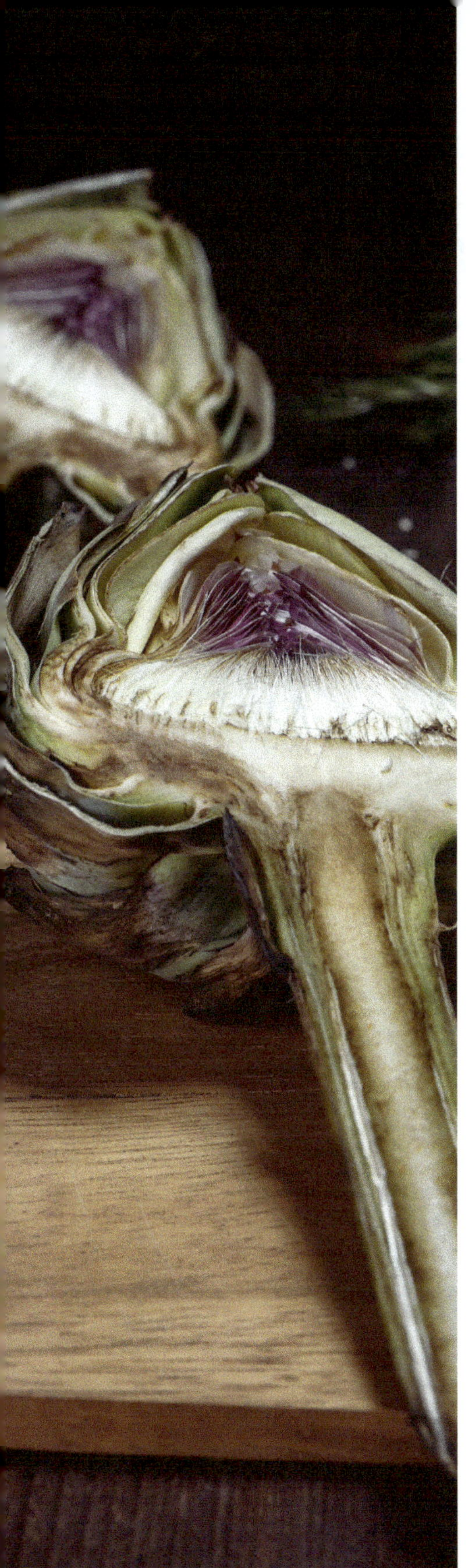

FRIED ARTICHOKES

To share

INGREDIENTS

4 artichokes
2 whole eggs
1/2 lemon squeezed
5-6 tablespoons of flour 0
salt
peanut oil for frying

DIRECTION

Clean the artichokes by removing the toughest leaves.

Slice them about half a centimeter thick and put them in water with lemon juice to keep them from darkening and to lose some of their bitterness.

Then dry them and pass them first in the flour, then in the beaten egg.

Fry them in hot oil and salt them.

FRIED COD

To share

INGREDIENTS

500 g (1lb 2oz) of desalted cod fillets
150 g (5 oz) of 00 flour
peanut oil for frying

DIRECTION

Remove the skin from the desalted cod, dry it and cut it into strips of about 3 cm.

Pass them in flour and cook for about 3-5 minutes in hot oil.

If necessary, add a pinch of salt

FRIED ZUCCHINI OR PUMPKIN FLOWERS

To share

INGREDIENTS

6 zucchini flowers
100 g (4 oz) of cooked ham
100 g (4 oz) of mozzarella
100 g (4 oz) of flour 0
100 g (4 oz) of sparkling water
salt
peanut oil for frying

DIRECTION

Clean the flowers by removing the inner part and wash them.

Cut the mozzarella and cooked ham into cubes, mix them and fill the flowers.

Prepare a batter with flour and sparkling water, pass the stuffed flowers in it and fry in hot oil. Salt after having drained them.

FRIED CRESPELLE CIOCIARE

To share

INGREDIENTS

500 g (1lb 2 oz) of flour 0
12.5 g (1 tablespoon) of brewer's yeast
325 g (12 oz) of warm water
30 g (1 oz) of fine salt
peanut oil for frying

DIRECTION

Dissolve the yeast in the water, add the flour and salt.

Knead well and leave to rise for about 2 hours.

Form small pizzas with your hands and fry them in hot oil.

Drain them and serve them

PRIMI

BREAD SOUP BELOW

The soup with bread below is a poor dish linked to the recovery of food, with stale bread being the protagonist, and to the natural rhythm of the vegetables, using seasonal vegetables and beans.

There is the use of the so-called crazy herbs: vegetables that grow spontaneously, including dandelion and chicory, which together with many other rural varieties, are the main ingredients to flavor many typical dishes of the place.

It is precisely from the skilful combination of the most diverse vegetables and beans that the balanced taste between freshness and body derives.

Serving size for 10 people

400 g of wild chicory (or spinach) (14oz)
400 g of wild chard (or chard) (14oz)
300 g of chickpeas (11oz)
300 g of lentils (11oz)
300 g of broad beans (11oz)
two medium-sized ripe tomatoes
two large carrots
a red onion
a stalk of celery
a clove of garlic
a chili pepper
twelve slices of stale bread
two liters of water (2 US quart)
200 g of grated pecorino (7oz)
salt and oil to taste.

DIRECTION

To make this soup, soak the dried legumes (chickpeas, lentils and broad beans) in warm water at least twelve hours beforehand.

At the time of preparation, clean and cut the fresh vegetables (chicory, chard, carrot, celery and tomatoes) into strips.

Separately, proceed by slicing the onion into thin slices and then frying it together with chili pepper and garlic.

When it turns golden, the fresh vegetables are slowly added until they are soft, then the legumes and water are added.

After having mixed everything, it is left to simmer on a low heat for at least ninety minutes, preferably in an earthenware container which must always remain covered.

When cooked, the soup must have a thick and creamy appearance and the water must have reduced by at least a third of its volume.

It is always advisable to taste the soup before serving to adjust the salt.

Lastly, proceed by placing a few slices of stale bread on the bottom of a container, pouring part of the soup over them, to be covered with other slices of bread.

By alternating the layers until all the ingredients are used up, a homogeneous and rather compact mixture is obtained.

You have to let everything rest for at least fifteen minutes before serving at the table, after having sprinkled with plenty of grated pecorino.

POLENTA

It is said that the origins of the Ciociara polenta date back to 1503, when Guglielmo Caetani, Duke of Sermoneta, returning home from exile, brought the corn seed with him.

The classic yellow flour was obtained from the corn, the basic ingredient of polenta.

A simple preparation that spread as a dish of the poor, shepherds and farmers, since corn flour and water were enough to make it.

Today it is considered a prized dish and appreciated by all!

POLENTA

TURNIP TOPS AND SAUSAGE

INGREDIENTS

Serving size for 4 people

For the polenta :

500 g of stone ground cornmeal (3 cups and half)
2 litres of water (2 US quart)
15 g of extra virgin olive oil (4 teaspoons)
1tbsp of coarse sea salt

For the sauce :

500 g of turnip tops (1lb 2oz)
1 clove of garlic
150 g of smoked provola (5oz)
4 sausages

DIRECTION

To make the polenta, place a thick-bottomed steel pot on the fire, pour the 2 liters of water, when the water is about to boil, add the salt, then pour in the flour, stirring with a wooden spoon (or with the special hazelnut stick called mattarello) keep cooking at a high temperature, stirring quickly. To avoid the formation of lumps also add the olive oil.

Continue stirring waiting for it to boil again, then reduce the heat to a minimum and continue cooking for 50 minutes on a gentle heat, stirring constantly, taking care not to make it stick to the bottom. After 50 minutes the polenta is ready; turn up the heat so that it detaches well from the pot, wait to see that it detaches well from the bottom. Now carefully invert the pan onto a round cutting board slightly larger than the diameter of the pan to unmold the polenta.

Wash the turnip tops thoroughly, remove the toughest stems, brown the garlic in a large pan then remove it and add the vegetables. Cook with a lid closed for the time to let the turnip tops deflate, then remove it and continue cooking, adding oil. Remove the casing from the sausages and cook them in the pan of turnip tops when they are almost cooked.

Pour the polenta into the serving dish, leaving a hole in the centre. Add the turnip tops with the sausages, cover with pieces of provola and cover to melt it a bit.

INGREDIENTS

Serving size for 4 people

500 g of pork ribs (1lb 2oz)

1/2 glass of white wine

700 g of tomato sauce (1lb 8 oz)

2 cloves of garlic

salt, chili pepper, pepper

celery

DIRECTION

Brown the garlic in the oil, add the ribs cut into small pieces, add the celery and after a few minutes add the wine and let it evaporate.

Season with salt, pepper and chili to taste, add a glass of water and cook over low heat until the water has evaporated, then add the tomato sauce and cook for another half hour.

Spread the hot polenta on a plate and season with the prepared sauce.

POLENTA
WITH PORK RIBS

Since now we already know how to make polenta, we did not consider it necessary to repeat the latter's recipe.

If not, please go back to the previous recipe.

E buon appetito!

CHICORY
SOUP
52

INGREDIENTS

Serving size for 4 people

500 g of beans (1lb 2oz)

500 g of field chicory
 (or chicory salad) (1lb 2oz)

500 g of homemade bread (1lb 2oz)

1 cotechino
 (or bacon or pork sausages)

1 carrots

1 onion

1 stalk of celery

1 chili pepper

40 g of parmesan (1 and half oz)

30 g of pecorino (1oz)

salt to taste

extra virgin olive oil

DIRECTION

In a saucepan, sauté the extra virgin olive oil, carrot, celery, onion, chili pepper, add the cotechino (or a piece of bacon or pork sausage), season by mixing with a wooden spoon, add the beans and cover everything with water and cook for about an hour and a half.

In the meantime, clean and blanch the chicory in salted water, drain by eliminating the excess water, then chop it finely and add it to the broth prepared with beans and pork, season for about 10 minutes.

Arrange the bread cut into slices in earthenware bowls and pour over the chicory with the beans, serve with a good dose of parmesan and pecorino.

TONNARELLI PASTA

Nothing so far has been more enjoyable in this process of creation than the impetuous duty to "unlearn".

What I thought I knew as a Chef, especially in terms of pasta, I had to unlearn and learn again, but this time from trusted hands, from a teacher who has known pasta for more than 80 years, a true "pastaia" (pasta maker)

I confess that even the technique with which the dough is rolled out, using the "mattarello", was an absolute novelty for me. A mere repetitive, mechanical action that requires a lot of practice. Practice which she obviously has in abundance and I, well, keep learning.

Thanks to this Lady with an affable character, brilliant sensitivity and, as a good Italian, endowed with a profound respect for tradition, we spent almost an entire morning making kilos and kilos of tonnarelli.

TONNARELLI CIOCIARA

INGREDIENTS

Serving size for 3 people

For the dough :

3 eggs

300 g of flour 00 (11oz)

fine salt to taste

For the sauce :

200 g of blanched peas (7oz)

200 g of porcini mushrooms (7oz)

300 g of sausage (11oz)

a stick of celery

half a shallot

a carrot

extra virgin olive oil

DIRECTION

Take the flour and distribute it on a pastry board or on a steel surface. Shell the eggs and add them in the center of the latter together with a pinch of fine salt. Beat the eggs with the help of a fork and gradually incorporate the flour inside.

When the mixture has thickened, proceed to knead by hand. Work the ingredients for about 10 minutes until you obtain a smooth and homogeneous loaf of fresh pasta.

At this point wrap it inside the transparent film and let it rest at room temperature for about 30 minutes. Once the time has elapsed, take ¼ of the dough and roll it out with the pasta machine or with a rolling pin until obtaining a thickness of about 5 millimeters.

With the pasta cutter in the "spaghetti alla chitarra" format of the fresh pasta machine, create the tonnarelli. Lay the tonnarelli created on a lightly floured work surface. Once the dough is finished, cover it with a cotton or linen cloth until ready to cook to prevent it from drying out.

Prepare a sauté with carrots, shallots and celery cut into small pieces. Add the sausage without casing, the mushrooms and peas and brown. Cook for about ten minutes and if necessary add a spoonful of hot water.

Cook the tonnarelli in boiling salted water for about 3 minutes and then toss them in a pan with the prepared sauce. Serve as desired with a sprinkling of black pepper and grated parmesan.

CECAPRETI PASTA

Why are they called Cecapreti? It should be emphasized that the name of this pasta is one of the oldest in Italy. They are also often called Strozzapreti, but this type of homemade pasta has different names depending on the region in which it is prepared.

In Lazio and in particular in the Ciociaria area, Cecapreti are very thick spaghetti made with water, egg and flour, with a particular consistency that requires careful chewing. There are various theories about the origin of the name.

The first tells us that priests were once accused (especially by the poor, often forced to fight hunger) of being beyond measure foodies and hence the wish that these men of the Church would choke on excessive eating.

Another legend instead speaks of the habit of housewives, a long time ago, of preparing and donating these big spaghetti to the priests, while the husbands (who returned from the countryside and from hard work) always found themselves eating the usual soup. The husbands therefore hoped, between one spoonful of soup and another, that some priest would remain choked.

CECAPRETI WITH RAGÙ SAUCE

INGREDIENTS

Serving size for 4 people

For the dough :

500 g of type 0 flour (1lb 2oz)
1 egg
200 g of water (1 cup)

For the ragù sauce :

500 g of ground beef (1lb 2oz)
1 pork sausages (optional)
100 g of pancetta (stretched) (4oz)(optional)
1 carrot
1 onion
1 rib of celery
1 clove of garlic
½ l of red wine (2 cups)
800 g of peeled tomato (1lb 4oz)
1 tablespoon of double tomato paste
4 tablespoons of Extra virgin olive oil (EVO)
salt to taste
rated pecorino romano to taste

DIRECTION

Sift the flour on a work surface and mix it with the egg and water. Work until you get a smooth dough hard. Wrap it in cling film and let it rest for 30 minutes. Break off a piece of dough and form one big spaghetto about 15 cm long. Continue until you run out of dough. Arrange the cecapreti on a dishcloth floured.

Take a saucepan, do a nice round of oil, add a clove of poached garlic and the chopped carrot, onion and celery and let simmer over low heat for at least 15 minutes. At this point if you want add the finely chopped bacon and the sausage by removing the casing and making it into small pieces inside the saucepan and brown. Remove the garlic clove and add the minced meat and brown, stirring constantly. When the meat has changed color uniformly, add the red wine and cook over high heat so as to quickly evaporate the alcoholic part. Add the double tomato paste and stir to dissolve it quickly. Now add the peeled tomato, mix and cook over low heat for about 1 hour or until the oil rises to the surface.

Serve and sprinkle with pecorino.

CECAPRETI
WITH
PORCINI MUSHROOMS

Since now we already know how to make cecapreti we did not consider it necessary to repeat the latter's recipe. If not, please go back to the previous recipe.
E buon appetito!

INGREDIENTS

Serving size for 5 people

500 g of cecapreti pasta (1lb 2oz)

For the sauce :

400 g of porcini mushrooms (14oz)
garlic
chili pepper
parsley
extravirgin olive oil
salt

DIRECTION

After having cleaned the mushrooms well and having separated the caps from the stems, cut them into fairly thin slices. Then, put them to fry for a few minutes in a pan, over a not too low heat, with oil, garlic and chili pepper, stirring frequently.

When they have dried, add a handful of parsley and season with salt. Depending on your taste, you can remove the chili and garlic before putting the mushrooms in the pan.

Put the cecapreti to cook in plenty of salted water and when cooked, put them in a pan together with the mushrooms.

Stir the pasta for a few minutes and then serve.

FINI FINI PASTA

The dish boasts a very long tradition (it appears on tables for the first time in 1500).

The 'fini fini', also called maccaruni, are still today one of the most popular first courses among the local population and many tourists.

These are handcrafted egg fettuccine. The dough is rigorously cut by hand with the help of a sharp knife in order to obtain a very thin product.

Fini fini can be enjoyed at any time of the year, but they become an indispensable dish during holidays, special occasions and during the so-called Ciociaro Carnival (in the second half of February).

The pasta, on these occasions, is served in the traditional local wooden plate which takes the name of scifa.

FINI FINI
WITH
WILD ASPARAGUS

INGREDIENTS

Serving size for 4 people

For the dough :

½ kg of flour (3cups and half)
4 eggs
salt as needed

For the sauce :

700 g of asparagus (1lb 8oz)
40 g of parmesan cheese (1 and half oz)
1 clove of garlic
salt
extra virgin olive oil

DIRECTION

Sift the flour so that there are no lumps and arrange it, in a fountain, on the work surface.

Then add a pinch of salt and the eggs in that order; knead for about ten minutes using the palms of your hands (the final dough must be smooth and very elastic). Make a small loaf, wrap it carefully in a damp cloth (alternatively you can use the traditional transparent kitchen film) and let it rest for about an hour. At this point you must, therefore, roll out the dough with the classic pasta machine (better known as grandma duck) or the rolling pin (called 'glie stenneture' in Ciociaria).

In the latter case, sprinkle the table with flour and knead the dough to give it a possibly round and thin shape. Wrap the dough around itself and proceed to cut it with a sharp knife.

Therefore, make the so-called 'fini fini' which, to be considered as such, must have a width of about ½ millimeter.

Clean the asparagus: remove the woody end from the stems by breaking them with your hands until the leaves appear. Wash them well under water to remove earthy residues and dab them gently.

Put the extra virgin olive oil in a rather large pan and let it flavor with the garlic clove. Add the asparagus and cook for 10-12 minutes, add salt towards the end.

Fill a pot with water and bring it to a boil. As soon as it comes to a boil, add a pinch of coarse salt and after a minute add the fini fini. The cooking time is very short (for about 3 minutes). Al dente cooking is very important.

When the pasta is al dente mix all in the pan carefully.

Complete with a sprinkling of grated parmesan, then serve immediately.

FINI FINI

WITH

TOMATO SAUCE

Since now we already know how to make fini fini, we did not consider it necessary to repeat the latter's recipe. If not, please go back to the previous recipe.

E buon appetito!

INGREDIENTS

Serving size for 4 people

500 g of fini fini pasta (1lb 2oz)
400 g of ripe tomatoes (14oz)
1 onion
1 chili pepper
grated pecorino
4 basil leaves
extra virgin olive oil
salt

DIRECTION

Take a pot and fill it with water, bring to a boil. Pour the ripe tomatoes inside, blanching them for about 5-7 minutes. Then drain them and let them cool. Remove the peel and the part with the seeds. If you have a vegetable strainer, use it, otherwise break up the tomato pulp with a knife.

Then take a pan and add a drizzle of extra virgin olive oil, the chili pepper (seed removed) and the finely chopped onion. Let the onion fry for 4-5 minutes and then add the tomato pulp. Add a pinch of salt and a few basil leaves. Brown the tomato pulp well over high heat for 3-4 minutes, as soon as they begin to soften, lower the heat and continue cooking for about 30 minutes.

Meanwhile, fill a pot with water and bring it to a boil. As soon as it comes to a boil, add a pinch of coarse salt and after a minute add the fini fini. The cooking time is very short (about 3 minutes), due precisely to the thin thickness of this pasta, however check the degree of cooking of the fini fini . Al dente cooking is very important.

Once the fini fini are cooked, drain them and pour them directly into the pan with the tomato sauce and sauté them with the sauce for a couple of minutes over high heat. In this way the fine ends will flavor themselves further.

Add a generous sprinkling of grated pecorino and finally garnish with a few fresh basil leaves.

GNOCCHI

"Thursday we will make gnocchi!" the Nonna constantly repeated to me. Thursday arrived and I had to miss my pasta class due to a mishap that required my full attention.

Realizing the hour, I called the Nonna to explain what had happened and to make her my proposal: "Can we make gnocchi tomorrow? Friday?". She answered me very directly to this question : "NO! Gnocchi are made on Thursday!".

Without understanding the reason for this blunt response, which remained echoing in my head, I then decided to search on internet, and below I will show you my surprising discovery.

The saying: "Thursday gnocchi, Friday fish, Saturday tripe" comes from the popular culture of the Lazio region.

The common use of preparing gnocchi on Thursday was due to the need to eat a substantial and caloric dish in view of the following day, Friday, which according to the Catholic tradition is "di magro", i.e. fasting or abstaining from the consumption of meat.

GNOCCHI
WITH
BOAR RAGÙ

INGREDIENTS

Serving size for 8 people

For the dough :

1 kg of potatoes (2lb 4oz)
1 kg of durum wheat semolina flour (2lb 4oz)
100 g of butter at room temperature (4oz)
100 g of grated Parmesan cheese (4oz)
2 whole eggs
1 nutmeg powder
a pinch of salt

For the ragù :

500 g of boar meat (1lb 2oz)
400 g of tomato sauce (14oz)
1 carrot
1 celery
1 onion
1 clove of garlic
3 bay leaves
1 sprig of rosemary
extra virgin olive oil (EVO) to taste
salt to taste
black pepper
1 glass of red wine

DIRECTION

Boil the potatoes in their skins.

Peel and weigh them, mash them and let them cool.

Combine butter pieces, eggs and then all the rest.

Knead well, make rolls and cut into cubes.

When you want to prepare the wild boar ragù, first of all chop the onion, celery and carrot and brown them in a saucepan with a drizzle of oil.

Then add the chopped garlic and let it simmer for about ten minutes on low heat.

Add the wild boar meat, the chopped rosemary, the whole bay leaves and mix by cooking for 10 minutes.

Deglaze with the red wine and, as soon as the alcoholic part has completely evaporated, add the tomato sauce.

Stir, add salt and pepper and cook with the lid on over low heat for at least 3 hours.

When the necessary time has elapsed, remove the lid and continue cooking for another half hour, so as to make the ragù drier.

Use wild boar ragù to season.

SAGNE PASTA

A dish loved by all, especially by Cicerone, the famous orator of ancient Rome, who discovered it in Arpino, the town where he was born.

Sagne, also known as maltagliati, is a very simple type of pasta, made from water and flour, cut irregularly. It is a poor dish, coming from the peasant tradition.

There are various condiments, but the beans, rigorously cannellini from Atina, are essential. The grandmothers cooked them in the typical terracotta pot, directly in the fireplace, in contact with the embers.

Some also add pancetta or bacon, others tomato sauce, still others opt for wild asparagus.

SAGNE WITH WILD ASPARAGUS AND WHITE BEANS

INGREDIENTS

Serving size for 4 people

For the dough

400 g of flour 0 (14oz)

approximately 250 ml of water (1 cup)

a pinch of salt

For the sauce

oil to taste

wild asparagus (or regular asparagus)

garlic

400 g of white beans (14oz)

salt and pepper

DIRECTION

Soak the white beans for about 12 hours.

Arrange the flour on a wooden plate. Add the warm water in which the salt was dissolved.

Start kneading until you get a compact and elastic compound.

Leave the dough to rest in a covered bowl for half an hour.

Then, roll out the dough, preferably with a rolling pin, about a millimeter thick.

Roll the dough to form a flattened roll and cut the sheet crosswise roughly, in the shape of a "priest's ear" or an "olive leaf".

Drain and rinse the cannellini beans and boil them for about 2 hours on a very low flame.

Cook the "sagne" in salted water for 4-5 minutes.

Fry the oil, garlic and asparagus in a pan, adding a drop of water.

Finally, pour the "sagne", the sauce, a ladleful of asparagus for each portion and some cooking water onto a plate so that the dish does not become too dry.

SAGNE
WITH
WHITE BEANS

INGREDIENTS

Serving size for 4 people

For the dough :

400 g of flour 0 (14 oz)

approximately 250 ml of water (1 cup)

a pinch of salt

For the sauce :

400 g of sagne (14 oz)

400 g of cannellini beans already boiled (14 oz)

4 tablespoons of extra virgin olive oil (EVO)

1 small onion

2 cloves of garlic

1 hot red pepper

1 rib of celery

salt to taste

800 g of tomato sauce (1lb 4oz)

DIRECTION

Arrange the flour ideally on a wooden board, but you can use any surface. Add the warm water in which the salt was dissolved.

Start kneading until you get a compact and elastic compound. Leave the dough to rest in a covered bowl for half an hour. Then, roll out the dough – preferably with a rolling pin – about a millimeter thick. Roll the dough to form a flattened roll and cut the dough roughly into squares.

Now prepare a fairly fine mince, with the onion, garlic, celery stick and hot pepper. Pour a drizzle of extra virgin olive oil into a pan and fry the sautéed mixture just prepared in the oil over low heat.

After a few minutes, add the tomato sauce to the sautéed mixture and cook for approximately 15-20 minutes.

After the time indicated above, add the already boiled white beans to the pan. Adjust with a pinch of salt, let everything flavor well for a few moments.

Bring the water to the boil in a 3 liters pot, once it boils, salt the water and put the pasta to boil. Leave to cook from the resumption of the boil for a few minutes.

As soon as the pasta has come to the surface, drain it directly into the pan with the sauce, if necessary add a ladle of the pasta cooking water, mix and let everything flavor well.

Serve sagne and beans with a drizzle of extra virgin olive oil.

SECONDI

BEEF STEW
WITH
POTATOES

INGREDIENTS

Serving size for 4 people

1 kg of beef (2lb 4 oz)

500 g of potatoes (1lb 2oz)

250 g of chopped onion, celery, carrot and bacon (9oz)

200 g of tomato sauce (7oz)

1 bouquet of thyme and bay leaf

1 clove of garlic

olive oil

salt

DIRECTION

Brown the chopped onion, celery, carrot and bacon in the oil.

Combine the meat cut into chunks, add the tomato sauce, the garlic, the sprig of thyme and bay leaf, and leave to simmer over a low heat for around 30 minutes.

Add the peeled and diced potatoes, cover with water, add salt and finish cooking slowly with the container covered for around 30 minutes.

CIOCIARIA RABBIT

INGREDIENTS

Serving size for 4 people

1 rabbit

2 fillets of anchovies or anchovies in oil

1 sprif of rosemary

1 pinch of marjoram

½ hot peppers

2 cloves of garlic

½ glass of white wine

½ glass of white wine vinegar

4 tablespoons of extra virgin olive oil (EVO)

salt to taste.

DIRECTION

Empty and cut the rabbit into chunks, season with salt and brown in a pan with oil.

When it is well browned, add chopped garlic, rosemary, marjoram and anchovy fillets and chili pepper; let it brown again, pour over half a glass of white wine and just under half a glass of vinegar.

Cover and simmer until the wine and vinegar have evaporated.

PORK LIVERS

WITH LAUREL

A DISH THAT REFUSES TO BE FORGOTTEN

Many had told us: "perhaps it is not the right season" (May), others told us maybe because this recipe was no longer very common.

How was it possible?

However, it was very important for us to obey our intuition and understand then that this dish was asking us to be remembered, to give life to that preparation, which was about to be forgotten. In this way tradition was the rule.

How? We left the idea of large stores behind and went to the butcher with his small business. When we got there, we even learned his name, that's how he introduced himself, with great alacrity: "I'm "Franco". Without wasting too much time, we made him aware of our request, and he undisguisedly made a gesture that showed the difficulty of what we requested, a couple of seconds of doubts in his mind, followed by: "can you come in a couple of days? but I can't assure you anything".

Precisely two days passed and we were there, with great expectations for our order, and, to our surprise, he had succeeded. Wonderful!

Furthermore, not only did he get it, but he did offer them as a gift.

Thank you Franco for your full attention and genuine kindness, a charitable and kind being!

Excited to finally have found everything, we took our way home and another beautiful surprise, yes, like magic, like serendipity, it happened: a large laurel plant crossed our path, it was right there next to a small street that we took by mistake, it gave us some of its leaves to complete this beautiful and delicious dish that we show you here.

INGREDIENTS

Serving size for 4 people

500 g of pork liver (1lb 2 oz)

300 g of pork rind softened in water (11oz)

5 fresh laurel leaves

40 g of lard (or 2 spoons of olive oil)

salt

pepper

DIRECTION

Clean the liver and cut it into pieces of about 30 g each.

Cut the net into squares of about 15 cm per side, line them up on the table, add salt and pepper and arrange a laurel leaf in the center of each one and a piece of liver on top.

Wrap them in bundles and brown them in a pan with the lard, turning them until they are cooked, golden and crunchy.

Serve them hot.

GOATLING
WITH ROSEMERY AND POTATOES

INGREDIENTS

Serving size for 3 people

800 g of goatling (1lb 4 oz)

5 large potatoes

2 lemons

oil, salt, pepper

DIRECTION

Sprinkle the goatling abundantly with salt and pepper, prick it here and there and put it to marinate the previous evening in a large container with oil, lemon juice and rosemary.

In the morning drain well, sprinkle with rosemary leaves, add the peeled and diced potatoes.

Arrange it on an oiled plate and roast in a very hot oven for 40/45 minutes, basting from time to time with the liquid from the marinade.

CIOCIARIA CHICKEN

INGREDIENTS

Serving size for 5 people

1 kg of chicken (2lb 4 oz)
300 g tomatoes (11 oz)
3 mixed peppers
1 piece of chili pepper
2 cloves of garlic
1/2 glass of white wine
1 tablespoon of oregano
salt to taste
extra virgin olive oil to taste.

DIRECTION

Put the garlic and chili pepper in a pan to fry in the oil. Brown the chicken in the pan, add salt and deglaze with white wine. In the meantime, remove the seeds and filaments from the peppers, cut them into pieces together with the tomatoes, add them to the chicken in the pan, mix well, add salt and cover with a lid. Leave to cook for about 40 minutes. Serve the chicken with a sprinkle of oregano.

SOUP OF COD

AND POTATOES

INGREDIENTS

Serving size for 5 people

1 kg of cod (2lb 4oz)
400 g of white potatoes (14oz)
300 g of tomato sauce (11 oz)
400 g of white onion (14oz)
1 sprig of parsley
stale bread to taste
4 cloves of garlic
1 glass of dry white wine
2 tablespoons of extra virgin olive oil
salt to taste
chili to taste

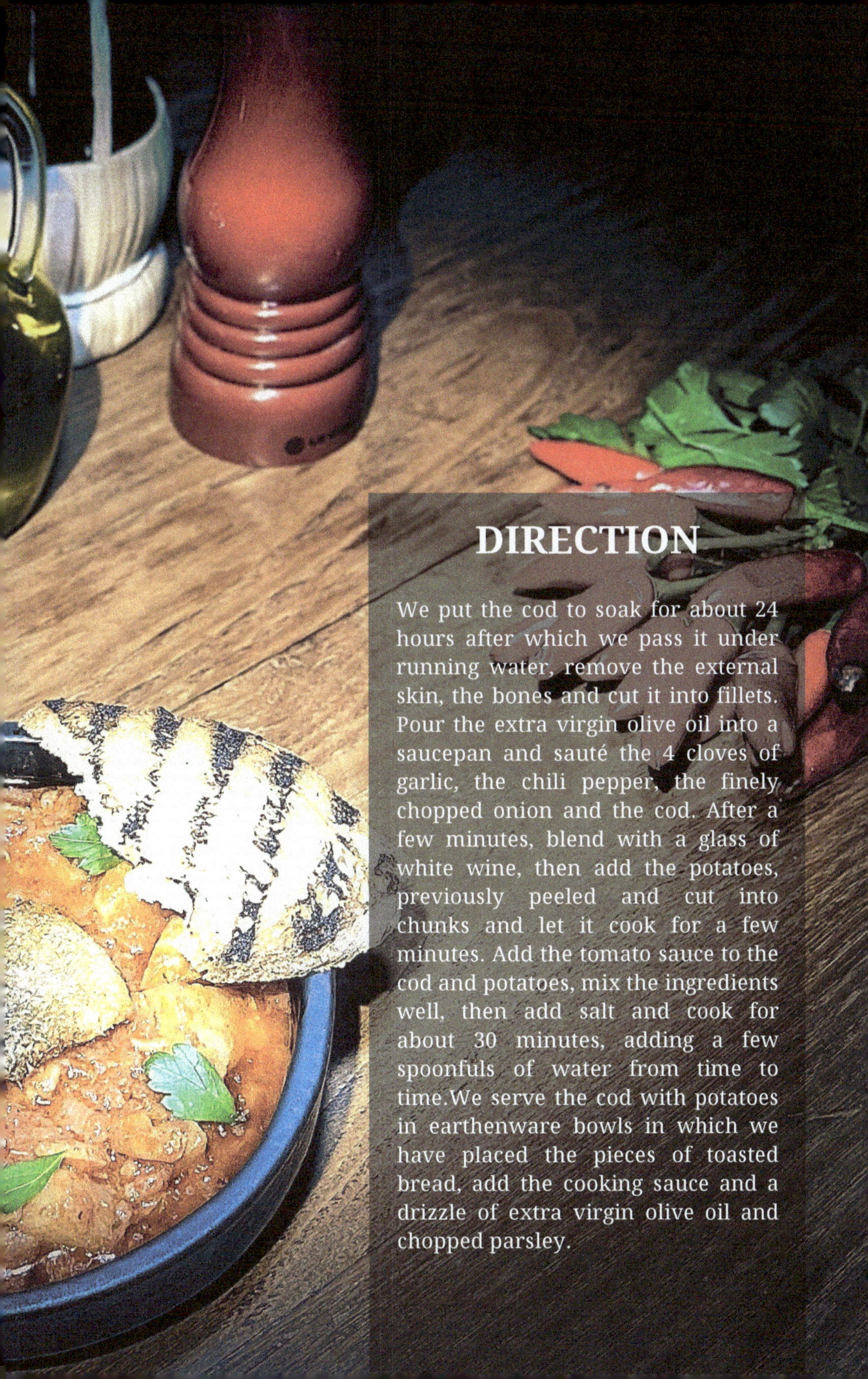

DIRECTION

We put the cod to soak for about 24 hours after which we pass it under running water, remove the external skin, the bones and cut it into fillets. Pour the extra virgin olive oil into a saucepan and sauté the 4 cloves of garlic, the chili pepper, the finely chopped onion and the cod. After a few minutes, blend with a glass of white wine, then add the potatoes, previously peeled and cut into chunks and let it cook for a few minutes. Add the tomato sauce to the cod and potatoes, mix the ingredients well, then add salt and cook for about 30 minutes, adding a few spoonfuls of water from time to time.We serve the cod with potatoes in earthenware bowls in which we have placed the pieces of toasted bread, add the cooking sauce and a drizzle of extra virgin olive oil and chopped parsley.

SAUSAGES

AND

TURNIP GREENS

INGREDIENTS

Serving size for 4 people

500 g of sausages (1lb 2 oz)
800 g of turnip broccoli (1lb 4 oz)
1 chili pepper
1 clove of garlic
1/2 glass of dry white wine
1 lard spoon
4 tablespoons of oil
salt

DIRECTION

Melt the lard in a pan, add the pricked sausages with a fork and three tablespoons of water. Cook over medium heat for about a quarter of an hour, turning the sausages from time to time. Drain and keep warm. In the meantime, clean and wash the broccoli, place them in the sausage cooking pan with the water that remains adhering to them, add oil, garlic and chili pepper, salt, cover and cook. Put the sausages back in the pan and sprinkle them with the wine, let it evaporate. Serve hot.

CIOCIARA TRIPE

INGREDIENTS

Serving size for 3 people

1 kg of veal tripe (2lb 4 oz)

1 onion

600 g of tomato sauce (1lb 5 oz)

1 carrot

1 stick of celery

2 bay leaves

1 clove of garlic

1/2 glass of wine (preferably red)

pecorino cheese

extra virgin olive oil

salt and pepper to taste

chili pepper (optional)

DIRECTION

Thinly slice the tripe, wash it very well under running water and drain it.

In a saucepan, possibly earthenware, fry the finely chopped herbs, the garlic and the bay leaves.

Add the tripe, brown it for a few minutes then blend it with the wine and let it evaporate.

Add the tomato sauce, season with salt and pepper and cook over low heat for at least 1 hour.

Bring to the boil, wetting from time to time with water and stirring often; before removing it from the heat, add some chili pepper if you like.

Stir and serve with plenty of grated pecorino.

CONTORNI

STUFFED POTATOES

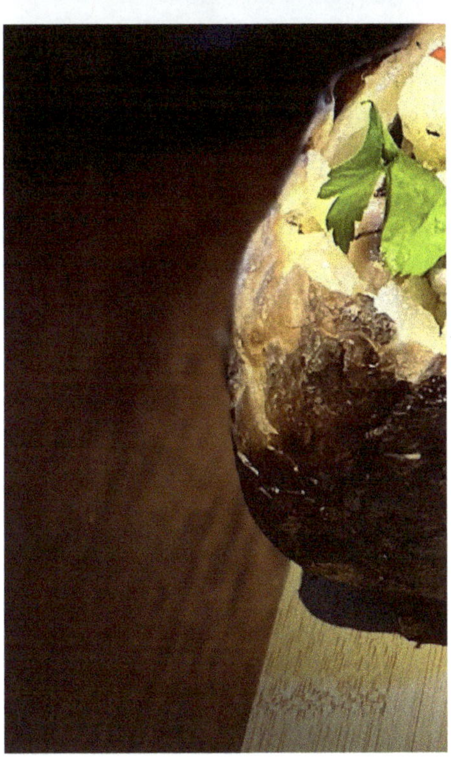

INGREDIENTS

Serving size : 1 potato a person

8 small potatoes

4 desalted anchovy fillets

a teaspoon of capers

a spoon of chopped parsley

a clove of garlic

extra virgin olive oil

DIRECTION

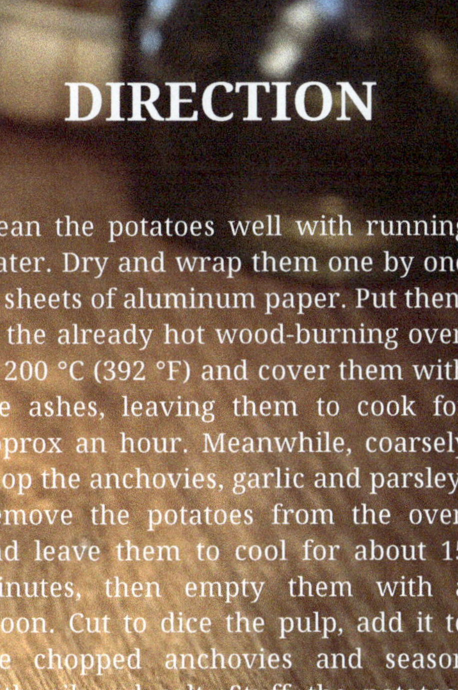

Clean the potatoes well with running water. Dry and wrap them one by one in sheets of aluminum paper. Put them in the already hot wood-burning oven at 200 °C (392 °F) and cover them with the ashes, leaving them to cook for approx an hour. Meanwhile, coarsely chop the anchovies, garlic and parsley. Remove the potatoes from the oven and leave them to cool for about 15 minutes, then empty them with a spoon. Cut to dice the pulp, add it to the chopped anchovies and season with oil and salt. Stuff the potatoes with the mixture prepared and put them in the oven for ten minutes. Serve hot.

PAN-FRIED
CHICORY
WITH
BEANS

INGREDIENTS

Serving size for 3 people

1 Kg of chicory (2lb 4 oz)

300 gr of boiled beans (10 oz)
(white or borlotti beans)

chili pepper

2 cloves of garlic

extra virgin olive oil

salt

DIRECTION

Wash the chicory by removing the roots and any bad leaves. Then after having washed it, scald it quickly in plenty of salted water.

Once the chicory has dried slightly, drain it in a colander (do not squeeze it). Form a ball and then cut it with a knife into smaller pieces. Continue to let it drain without squeezing it.
Take a large saucepan and add a little oil, some chili pepper and two cloves of garlic. Sauté the garlic for 3-4 minutes. Then add the boiled beans. Stir and let them brown for a few minutes before adding the chicory.

Add a couple of glasses of water, season with salt and continue cooking over low heat for about 20 minutes, with the lid closed. Remove the lid from time to time and stir to check the degree of cooking. The soupy part must always be present and in the end it must be sufficiently thick. Turn off and serve.

CABBAGE
AND
POTATOES

INGREDIENTS

Serving size for 3 people

600 g of potatoes (1lb 4 oz)
400 g of cabbage leaves (14 oz)
1 medium onion
50 g of bacon (2 oz)
oil and salt.

DIRECTION

Wash the leaves, peel the potatoes and cut them into chunks.

Put the potatoes in the watercold, bring it to the boil, salt and add the leaves.

Leave to cook for about 45 minutes.

In a pan fry the sliced onion and bacon cut into strips over low heat, which will have to lose its fat without drying out.

As soon as they are cooked, drain the potatoes and the leaves and put them in the pan; while season them, break them up coarsely and mix well.

STUFFED ENDIVE

INGREDIENTS

Serving size : 1 endive per person

1 head of lettuce (endive)

25 g of bread (1 oz)

parsley to taste

half small clove of garlic

4 olives

2 capers

3 anchovies

olive oil

DIRECTION

Choose tender and rather small heads of endive.

Open them in the shape of a rose and salt them.

Meanwhile you have to prepare a mixture of breadcrumbs seasoned with parsley, garlic, olives, capers, anchovies and a little oil.

Place a handful of this mixture in the center of the endive head and tie it.

Cook in a pan with oil and a little water over moderate heat.

STUFFED CORNETTO PEPPER

INGREDIENTS

Serving size for 2 people

4 Cornetto peppers(or any kind of pepper)
300 g of sheep ricotta (10 oz)
3-4 pork sausages
100 g of salted ricotta (4 oz)
1/2 glass of white wine
extra virgin olive oil q.s.
salt and pepper to taste

DIRECTION

142

Clean the peppers by removing the stalk and eliminating the seeds and any residues inside.

Boil water in a large pot.

Blanch the peppers for about ten minutes.

In the meantime, crumble the sausage and cook it in a pan over medium/high heat, blending it with the wine.

When the sausage is ready, compose the filling by mixing together the ricotta, the sausages with their sauce and the grated salted ricotta, taste and add salt and pepper if necessary.

Fill the peppers, previously left to dry, with the stuffing using a pastry bag or more simply with a spoon.

Put in the oven at 356 °F for about 25/30 minutes adding extra virgin olive oil.

ROSEMARY FLAVORED CHICKPEAS SOUP

INGREDIENTS

Serving size for 5 people

Half kg of dried chickpeas (1lb 2 oz)
2 cloves of garlic
salt to taste
extra virgin olive oil q.s.
1 sprig of fresh rosemary
water to taste

DIRECTION

First, soak the dried chickpeas the night before, and let them soak overnight. Brown the garlic cloves in a little oil, add the chickpeas after having rinsed them from the water where they have been soaking all night. Add the sprig of fresh rosemary and the water and cook for at least an hour. Stir occasionally and add salt after cooking. Serve still hot and if you like you can add a drizzle of raw extra virgin olive oil, chili pepper or Parmesan.

DOLCI

GUARCINO
AMARETTI

The production of Amaretto di Guarcino has been going on for about a century. The story goes that the recipe for these almond soft biscuits was donated by an old friar, in gratitude to those who, after kilometers and kilometers of walking, stopped in the town of Guarcino, who had offered him food and welcome hospitality.

INGREDIENTS

Serving size for 10 people

300 g of icing sugar (10 oz)
200 g of peeled sweet almonds (7 oz)
wafer papers for dessert
4 egg whites
20 g of bitter almonds (¾ oz)

DIRECTION

Chop the almonds, both varieties, in the mixer; transfer the chopped mixture into a bowl and mix it with the sugar. Whip the egg whites very stiff and add them, little by little, to the almond mixture, mixing very delicately so as not to disassemble the mixture. Line a baking tray with the appropriate baking paper, distribute the wafer papers well spaced on it, then put a spoonful of the prepared mixture on each one, giving it a slightly oval shape. Put the Guarcino amaretti in the oven for about half an hour at 356 °F, or in any case let them cook until they are golden brown. At the end of cooking, take them out of the oven and let them cool. Then gently remove them from the pan by detaching them from the parchment paper and serve them.

CIAMBELLINE RUZZE

Wine donuts are simple, dry and very crumbly biscuits. They were always prepared where wine was made, where butter was considered a wealth while oil was abundant, and desserts were prepared only for holidays. They were dry biscuits because they had to keep for a long time and precisely because they had to last a long time they made a lot of them. Ruzze donuts are very aromatic and are prepared at every occasion of the year. They can be enjoyed soaked in white wine at the end of lunch but also as a snack and at any time of the day because they are super delicious.

INGREDIENTS

Serving size for 10 people

500 g of 00 flour (1 lb 2 oz)
250 g of sugar (9 oz)
a pinch of salt
1 and 1/2 glass of white wine (or red wine)
1/2 cup of olive oil
1 teaspoon yeast (optional)
1 tablespoon of anise seeds

DIRECTION

Arrange the flour in a bowl with the sugar, a pinch of salt, the anise seeds, the olive oil and the white wine and, if you like, the yeast into it.
Mix all the ingredients well until you get a firm but quite soft dough.
Take some pieces of dough, cut them into strings and form some not too big donuts.
Roll them in granulated sugar.
Arrange the ruzze donuts on an oiled cookie sheet or on parchment paper and place in a preheated oven at 340 °F for about 40-45 minutes, until the surface is golden brown.

NONNA'S
CAKE
154

INGREDIENTS

Serving size for 8 people

4 eggs
250 grams of sugar (9 oz)
the skin of a grated organic lemon
a glass of milk
a glass of seed oil
1 bite of yeast (16 gr)(1 tablespoon)
about 400 grams of flour 00 (14 oz)

DIRECTION

Beat for at least 5 minutes with the electric or hand whips, the eggs with sugar, then add the oil and milk and mix with a wooden spoon. Also grate the lemon peel. Place flour and sifted yeast at this point: the mixture must be very soft (otherwise add some more milk). Grease with butter and flour a 20 or 22 cm barrel bowl. Bake in a static oven at 356 °F for 50 minutes, or until the needle comes out dry from the inside of the cake.

WILD
CHERRY
PIE

INGREDIENTS

Serving size for 10 people

FOR THE SHORTCRUST PASTRY :

200 g of granulated sugar (7 oz)
3 eggs (2 whole + 1 yolk)
125 g of sunflower seed oil (4½ oz)
half sachet of baking powder
the grated peel of 1/2 lemon
1 vanilla pod
500 g of 00 flour (1 lb 2 oz)

FOR THE CHERRY JAM :

300 gr of wild cherries
(weighed with seeds) (10 oz)

140 g of sugar (5 oz)

DIRECTION

First of all prepare the jam. Take the wild cherries, remove the stems, wash and dry them. After weighing them, also remove the pits. Take a saucepan and pour the cherries with the sugar inside. Put everything on the fire and cook for about an hour from the start of the boil. During cooking, everything must be turned continuously to prevent the jam from sticking to the bottom and from time to time to remove the foam that forms on the surface. The jam will be ready once it becomes glossy and of the desired consistency. It is necessary to let it cool before using it in the pie.

Place the flour on the table or a bowl, making a hole in the center and add all the ingredients to make the dough. Work quickly. Divide the dough into two parts (3/4 and 1/4) and roll out the largest dough. Grease with butter and flour a pan of about 25 cm in diameter and line it internally with the previously rolled out dough. Lay the jam on top, then roll out the remaining dough (1/4) by cutting it into strips with a knife . Place the strips on the jam by crossing them and forming diamond shapes. Fold the edges back on themselves blocking the ends of the strips. Bake at 170°C (338 °F) for 40 minutes.

EASTER CAKE

In popular tradition, the Easter Pigna is prepared in the week before Easter. All the families get to work preparing a cake that looks so much like panettone. Enriched inside with pieces of candied fruit, vanilla or anise seeds, it acquires a wonderful scent. The Easter Pigna can be kept for a long time, for several days, always remaining as fragrant as when it was freshly made.

INGREDIENTS

Serving size for 1 cake

320 gr (12 oz) of flour 00
7,5 gr (1 and half teaspoons) brewer's yeast
2 whole eggs
110 g (4 oz) of granulated sugar
the grated peel of half lemon
34 g (3 tablespoons)of extra virgin olive oil
34 g (3 tablespoons)of melted butter
1 table spoon of sambuca
1 table spoon of anise
6 g (1 teaspoon) of anise seeds
1/2 pod of vanilla
60 gr (4 tablespoons)of mixed candied fruit
in small pieces (citron, cherries, orange peel)
20 g (2 tablepoons) of raisins
60ml (4 tablespoons) of warm water
colored sprinkles to decorate
icing glaze (1 egg white + 1 tablespoon sugar)

DIRECTION

FIRST DOUGH :

Mix 100 g (4 oz) of flour with 60 ml (4 tablespoons) of warm water in which 2.5 g (half teaspoon) of brewer's yeast have been dissolved.

The dough must be soft. Leave to rise until doubled in volume. Then proceed with the second dough.

SECOND DOUGH :

Place the 2 whole eggs with the sugar and lemon peel and mix well with an electric mixer.

Then add the first dough made, plus the other 5 g (1 teaspoon) of dry brewer's yeast.

Mix well with an electric mixer. Now add all the other ingredients by mixing with your hands.

Place everything in a warm place so that the volume of the dough doubles. Then take a buttered and floured tray and placing the dough inside .

Leave to rise again in a warm place until doubled in volume. Oven at 150°C for 50 minutes.

Before baking, brush the cake with the prepared icing and decorate with colored sprinkles. Refresh for a few minutes.

CRESPELLE CIOCIARE

WITH RAISINS

If they're not at the table, it's not Christmas. In a typical Ciociaria menu, at Christmas, simple "crespelle" fried in boiling oil, with raisins and sugar are an indispensable tradition. It is a poor dessert, made with simple ingredients, which refers to the most ancient tradition of the Ciociaria table.

INGREDIENTS

Serving size for 10 people

500 g flour 0 (4 cups)

250 g raisins (1 cup)

12.5 g brewer's yeast (2 teaspoons)

325 g warm water (1 and half cup)

30 g of fine salt (1 tablespoon)

peanut oil

sugar to taste

DIRECTION

Dissolve the yeast in the water, add the flour, salt and raisins.

Knead well and leave to rise for about 2 hours.

Make small pizzas with your hands and fry in hot oil.

Drain and sprinkle them in sugar.

TIPS

1. To adjust the acidity level of the ragù, you can add milk a little at a time almost at the end of cooking.

2. Once the fresh homemade pasta starts to float, it means it's ready.

3. To obtain a fantastic creamy sauce in fresh pasta dishes, simply take a little of the pasta cooking water and mix it separately with olive oil.

4. If you don't want to buy dried beans and chickpeas, a valid option are those that are already cooked. Better to buy them in glass jars to make sure that the legumes are whole.

5. If you don't want to make tomato sauce at home but buy one that's already made, the important thing is to buy a quality one that doesn't already have spices inside (garlic, basil, etc.).

6. Since wild boar meat is very strong, it is necessary to treat it in advance. At least 24 hours before cooking, put it to marinate with oil and lemon.

7. As for the meat stew, an idea may be to cook it in a pressure cooker for at least half an hour. In this way you will obtain a very soft meat and the cooking times will be halved

Have you noticed our ceramic plates that serve as a canvas ?

From our homemade ceramic tableware to each of the culinary preparations,   these are the result of our craftsmanship.

Plates and bowls artistically made by Lucia , all Nonna's recipes translated with my hands in the most fair way, are part of this beautiful symbiosis.

The oil used in all our recipes is extra virgin olive oil from organic farming, produced for over 100 years by Lucia's family.

Golden streets that adorn,
with echoes of light,
flowery balconies on stone facades

Streets that keep in their essence
the history of Cicerone and Gaio Mario

Narrow streets that use stone arches as loudspeakers,
steps that echo in the valley that covers it.
Are like giant steps.

Streets of lights,
lights that are slowly extinguished at sunset.
A pink, purple, gold twilight.
Say goodbye every day.